# NAJAF CHARTER

## FOR THE CONSERVATION, RESTORATION, AND REHABILITATION OF CITIES, URBAN AREAS, HISTORIC-HERITAGE MONUMENTS, AND THE NATURAL HERITAGE PROTECTION

**The Preservation Center of Heritage and Identity of Iraqi Cities**

www.pchiic.ieefoundation.org

**NOTICE TO THE READER**
The Publisher has taken reasonable care in the preparation of this book, but makes no expressed or implied warranty of any kind and assumes no responsibility for any errors or omissions. No liability is assumed for incidental or consequential damages in connection with or arising out of information contained in this book. The Publisher shall not be liable for any special, consequential, or exemplary damages resulting, in whole or in part, from the readers' use of, or reliance upon, this material.

Najaf charter for the conservation, restoration, and rehabilitation of cities, urban areas, historic-heritage monuments, and the natural heritage protection.

The Preservation Center of Heritage and Identity of Iraqi Cities, 2020.

www.pchiic.ieefoundation.org

ISBN-13: 9798707119286

# Abstract

This charter will be formulated based on international charters on urban heritage and religious cities, which have been prepared by the International Council on Monuments and Sites (ICOMOS) and United Nations Educational, Science and Cultural Organization (UNESCO). The preservation of the identity of Iraqi cities is done through three basic themes:

- Keep all the heritage places of the Iraqi cities, with its sense of the patterns of urban and distinctive heritage, and maintain it from erosion and extinction, and in accordance with the international standards.

- The development of standards and regulations that govern the process of designing buildings to be built in the old cities of Iraq and in line with the features and patterns inherent architectural and heritage of the city.

- Preserving the traditional renewable energy systems and sustainability principles in the heritage buildings of the old cities of Iraq, and collect, disseminate and promote research in the area of energy conservation and sustainable development in those buildings. In addition to that, protection of natural heritage and distinctive ecosystems.

We hope that this charter will be model regulations in order to preserve the identity of all Iraqi cities.

The Preservation Center of Heritage
and Identity of Iraqi Cities
*www.pchiic.ieefoundation.org*

1

# Preface

The most important characteristic of this charter is that, it is considered the first comprehensive document of its kind to be accomplished in Iraq concerned with the Iraqi city and working to preserve its heritage and identity. Substantially, it is an elaborate Iraqi product with a sober global vision. In this charter, the features of the dialectical relationship among man, place and time, have been defined in accurate expressions, simplicity and clarity, as well as, thus the reader and whoever follows the provisions of this charter can touch in it the human and juridical language that affirms the right of societies and peoples to preserve their heritage and cultural achievement as well as, preserve their memory from extinction.

This charter bears the name of **Al-Najaf**, because it is the city that witnessed at the beginning of 2011, the first consultative sessions in which the issue of identity and heritage of Iraqi cities was discussed and what they suffer from obliteration and removal as a result of many factors and how to preserve them. And an elite of Iraqi experts and specialists joined these. The sessions that led to the need to prepare a charter concerned with this matter. In 2013, efforts paid off with the issuance of the first version of the Najaf Charter, which would serve as an integrated road map for all concerned in the administrations of the city affairs, decision-makers, in addition to planners, engineers,

academics, researchers and those interested in the identity and distinctive heritage of each city. Najaf city, served as a starting point for serving all cities in Iraq.

Seven years after the issuance of the first version, and through in-depth studies, academic research and a series of specialized conferences and seminars, the second version of the charter was issued in 2020, which included important qualitative additions and included more than a number of axes that dealt with several issues related to conservation.

This charter does not stop the development of the city or be an obstacle to the spread of the manifestations of modernity in it, but rather works to find a scientific and balanced solution to the dialectical relationship between authenticity, what it carries in memory, cultural heritage and modernity as a human and technical need imposed by the laws of life, so this charter comes to govern all these activities in the city space, with the rules of preserving the identity, as same as to all the cities in the world.

## 1. Introduction

Local architectural heritage occupies a special place in the hearts of people. It gets the pride of all generations, as a distinctive and attractive product. Although it is a man-made heritage, it is also the product of time! It would be unfair if this human heritage do not receive enough care and attention, and if those traditional

harmonies and rhythms, which are considered public cultural properties, are not kept.

The importance of local urban heritage lies in being the expression of a specific society's culture and civilization as related to its land. At the same time, it is a representation of the cultural diversity of different societies in the world.

The local architecture represents the natural traditional methods taken by the communities according to their lifestyle. It is a result of a continuous process of developing ongoing necessary modifications and adaptations in response to the subjective needs of people and the objective factors of environment. Remaining of this tradition under the continuous threat by the forces of globalization and renewal, would lead to melting and vanishing of local distinctive identities!. The way these forces gather and interact constitutes a dilemma that must be identified and resolved by the communities, as well as by the governments, planners, architects, conservatives and multi-disciplinary specialists teams.

This clarifies the importance of conserving the cultural heritage of Iraqi cities, and the identity distinct for each. It also clarifies the need to move quickly with all available means to stop all types of distortion to all Iraqi cities urban fabric, and to limit the introducing of strange architectural styles, irrelevant to the every

city's cultural identity, that are widely increasing recently, threatening this identity.

The conversation of cultural property, including the architectural heritage as a national wealth, is considered as a national responsibility. Based on Clause 113 of the Iraqi constitution, Law no. 55 of 2002, which says: (Monuments, archaeological sites, traditional structures, manuscripts and historical coins are considered as national wealth ....), it is not permitted to deal with architectural heritage without the approval of the related archaeological authority. Thus, there is an urgent need to activate and reinforce legal law and bylaws, unifying the efforts of related governmental departments, and educating the citizens to their national responsibility of protecting the identity of the city, its outstanding urban historical architecture, and the Iraqi spiritual and physical heritage, all in accordance with the standards set in international charters, and related tools and mechanisms for protecting historical heritage.

The Preservation Center of Heritage and Identity of Iraqi Cities (PCHIIC), presents this charter as a technical document that represents the summary of the work of a team of experts, as it is considered a clear roadmap for dealing with the cultural heritage of Iraqi cities and preserving their distinctive identity, in addition to that, this charter is subject to growth and

development according to the nature and requirements of each city And under the supervision of specialized experts.

## 2. Principles and Objectives

To conserve the historical identity of Iraqi cities, represented by its heritage buildings and outstanding urban fabric, like traditional world cities had done, and to use the approved international urban renewal strategies adopted in developed cities of the world, the following actions should be considered:

**1-** To Commit to international treaties and charters adopted by the (UNESCO) and the International Council on Monuments and Sites (ICOMOS), apply their mechanisms in dealing with urban heritage around the world, and revive the agreements to conserve the legacy of cities, including the Iraqi cities, such as "The Venice Charter" which was signed by Iraq at the end of the twentieth century, in coordination with UNESCO and ICOMOS.

**2-** To conserve all historic urban areas in the Iraqi Cities, with all their distinctive architectural and traditional types, and to maintenance them of erosion and extinction, in accordance with the adopted international standards, laws and charters.

**3-** To identify the borders of the historic centre of each city (the Old City), thus to determine the applicable laws and instructions relate to it, which are different from those related to the rest of the city, as applied in the global historical cities.

**4-** To set rules governing land uses in the Old City, to ensure they have no adverse impact on the heritage identity of the city and its spiritual, or holy, or historic sacredness, and to work on the immediate cessation of the demolition works in traditional areas.

**5-** To preserve traditional renewable energy systems and the principles of sustainability adopted in the city's heritage buildings.

**6-** To work with the legislative authority to issue the necessary legislation to consider heritage areas as "protected heritage areas" having special systems.

**7-** To include religious buildings within global maintenance standards, and to declare them as archaeological sites in official newspapers, in all Iraqi provinces, paying great attention to the importance of the Holy Shrines, worship places and holy monuments, and its role it the society life, stopping any project

or infill within the historic city centre that might cause a bad impact on this importance.

**8-** To set or develop regulations and standards that govern the urban planning, urban design and architectural design of new areas and buildings during urban expansion taking place in the city, in line with the genuine features and architectural styles of the Old City, including them in the master plan and detail plan.

**9-** To educate the new generation with the value of the city and its civilization depth, to enhance their consciousness to its importance to the present and the future, raising their pride of it, and to urge them to pursue policies that would preserve their heritage. That can be achieved through educational events for different schools in the city for example, and declaration of certain Day of the city to celebrate and define its importance.

**10-** To establish a consultative centre having a group of experienced specialists, providing advice for all parties in need, especially for those who are concerned with urban planning, and preparation of master plan of the city. An educational school would be associated with this centre, having workmanship professionals who work with local traditional materials in the city. This school can be responsible for the acts of conservation,

preservation, restoration, and renovation of traditional fabric and archaeological heritage areas, in integration with other institutes concerned with crafts & heritage building.

**11-** To start implementing a development plan for a small part of the historical centre of the city as a model, according to international standards, laws and charters to have a feedback regarding the positive and negative points. Academic thesis for architecture schools and urban planning students can be utilised in this field.

**12-** To involve local communities in urban heritage preservation programs and projects, to find the appropriate formulas for that, and to take advantage of the rehabilitation of urban heritage buildings for the daily life of the city in residential, tourist or cultural uses.

## 3. Terms of the Charter

### 1ST item: Conservation at the City level
**Article (A):**
The concept of the (historical monument) is not limited to single architectural work, but it is also related to the urban fabric of urban settlements, in reference to a particular civilization,

distinctive evolution or historic event. Applying it is not limited as well to the great works of art, but also to the ordinary works of the past that were gaining  traditional character over the time.

## Article (B):

Present works within local buildings or settlements must take care of their cultural values and traditional identity. They should aim for the successful protection to the local heritage, which is depending on level of social involvement and support, continuous use and maintenance.

## Article (C):

Interference in local structures should be done in a way that respects and keeps the site safety, its relation with natural and cultural environment, and the relation between each building with the others. The conservation plan should determine which buildings must be conserved, which should be preserved under certain circumstances and which, under quite exceptional circumstances, might be expendable. Before any intervention, existing conditions in the area should be thoroughly documented. The conservation plan should be supported by the local residents of the historic area.

## Article (D):

Adaptation and reuse of local structures must be done through a method that respects the structure's safety, character and shape, while complying with the decent living standards and international standards ensuring continuity and cultural communication.

## Article (E):

In order to work more efficiently, it is important to maintain the historic towns, and other historical urban areas, as an outcome of integration of consistent economic, urban and social policies, along with urban and regional planning at all levels, all included in the developing plans.

## Article (F):

Contemporary functions and activities within the city or the historical urban area must be consistent with their personality. Adaptation of these areas for contemporary life requires careful attention, and development to people's activities, with the provision of all necessary technical and cultural infrastructures.

## Article (G):

Traffic inside a historic town or urban area must be controlled. Parking areas must be planned so that they do not damage the

historic fabric or its environment, nor they interrupt pedestrian paths.

## Article (H):

Rehabilitation projects and the rebuilding of heritage areas must be placed within the urban planning scheme that includes all areas of the city, with attention to the distinctive features of those areas and their common uses.

## 2nd Item: Conservation at the Neighborhood level
## Article (A):

The participation of the population is important to the success of the city's identity maintaining program.  Conservation of cities and urban areas begins with the care of people in the first place, in addition to the care of residential complexes.

## Article (B):

Housing improving and maintenance of old or collapsed residential buildings must be one of the core objectives to keep the identity of the city, including the strengthening of the of neighbourhood concept and social cohesion, and raising the population. It may require some government administrative procedures to purify the distinctive urban areas from improper trades and activities that accumulate in them making them

unsuitable for their original residents who displace accordingly to new areas, and the neighbourhood links become weak as a result.

## 3rd Item: Conservation at the Religious Buildings level

Great attention must be given to holy shrines, religious buildings and all worship places, as spiritual and material legacy, being the key landmark in the city, to its residents and visitors. This landmark must be treated according to the international regulations of conservation and maintenance.

## 4th Item: Conservation at Buildings level

**Article (A):**

The monument is a non-isolated part of its history and environment. It is not permitted to remove all or part of any monument.

**Article (B):**

The process of restoration is a highly specialized one, aiming to conserve and reveal the aesthetic and historic value of the monument. It should respect original materials and authentic documents. The restoration in any case must be preceded and followed by an archaeological and historical study of the monument.

## Article (C):

Where traditional techniques prove to be inadequate, the consolidation of a monument can be achieved by the use of any modern technique for conservation and construction, the efficiency of which had been shown by scientific data and proved by experience, in a hidden way that do not harm the distinctive appearance of the monument.

## Article (D):

Replacements of missing parts must integrate harmoniously with the whole, but at the same time must be distinguishable from the original, so that restoration does not falsify the artistic or historic evidence.

## Article (E):

The process of rehabilitating historical buildings and centers in cities, acquires great importance in the field of stimulating tourism investment for these cities and the subsequent economic prosperity and growth of financial returns for the local community, which would be an encouraging factor in preserving the material heritage and historical features of the city.

## 5$^{th}$ Item: Conservation at the Details & Decorative Works level

Subjects as paintings, sculptures, or decorations which form an integral part of the monument cannot be removed, being parts of it.

## 6$^{th}$ Item: Conservation at Renewable Energy Systems & Sustainability Principles level

### Article (A):

The energy systems and sustainability criteria in traditional buildings must be maintained.

### Article (B):

Sustainability criteria that were adapted in heritage buildings and traditional cities of organic compacted fabric should be determined, in order to encourage to adopt and utilize them in contemporary building systems.

## 7$^{th}$ Item: Preserving the natural heritage, ecosystems and their constituent elements

The natural areas located within the urban fabric of cities or those located in or near adjacent areas, which are distinguished by their unique natural features and their unique geological and physiographic formations, in addition to containing all the

elements of biological diversity and their distinctive ecosystems, are considered a natural heritage that must be preserved and protected from tampering, removal and change. As well as the various types of damages that may be caused to it or to one of its constituent elements should be stopped.

Any removal of part or all of those areas and the disturbance of their natural balances due to the expansion of cities or the expansion of the various activities related to them, is considered a loss of one of the most important types of societal, national and human heritage.

The protection and maintenance of natural areas is done by preserving all its elements and not introducing any kind of activities that disrupt the normal natural patterns or inserting any foreign element into its harmonious and balanced natural system.

## 8<sup>th</sup> Item Documentation, Recording and Publication

**Article (A):**

In all works of preservation, restoration or excavation, there should always be precise documentation in the form of analytical and descriptive reports, illustrated with drawings and photographs, including every stage of the works of clearing, strengthening, rearrangement and integration. Technical and methodological articles prepared during the course of the work,

should   be included. These record should be placed in the archives of a public institution and made available to researchers. It is also recommended that these reports be published.

## Article (B):

The process of documenting and inventorying, including the documentation of construction methods, is considered essential for the success of the process of rehabilitating, maintaining and building cultural heritage, ensuring the protection of its outstanding universal value and fulfilling the test of its authenticity and safety conditions. Documentation and its regular updating, making the most of the capabilities offered by modern technologies, is an essential element in managing any site.

## Article (C):

Every country, through institutions qualified for this purpose, to issue an list of the monuments eligible for preservation, not only ancient ones, but also important ones to the memory of the community,  being related to historical events, famous persons, urban events or special stages. The list to be with pictures and explanatory notes. Copies of such publication to be deposited to UNESCO and relevant organizations.

## Article (D):

The record should include the name of the monument or the group of buildings, a special code for reference, date of the written record, name of registry organization, various references of concerned building records, reports, text and illustration documents.

## Article (E):

New records must refer to all new sources of information that are not collected directly from the monument, group of buildings or the site which they are surrounded by.

## Article (F):

The records must include the following information:

1- Pattern, shape and dimensions of the building, monument or location.

2- Internal and external features, conveniently, for the monument or group of buildings or site.

3- The nature and quality of cultural, artistic and scientific significance of the heritage and its components.

4- Materials, main parts, construction, ornaments, or decoration.

**5-** Services and mechanical equipment and structures.

**6-** Attached structures, gardens and topographic and natural site.

**7-** Traditional and modern techniques and skills used in construction and maintenance.

**8-** Evidences proving the creation date, creator, owner, the original design, use, expansion and decoration.

**9-** Evidences citing the sequential history of uses and events associated with it, ornamental and structural changes and the impact of external forces of human and natural resources.

**10-** History of management, maintenance and repairs.

**11-** Typical members or models of construction or site materials.

**12-** Assessment of the current state of heritage value.

**Article (G):**
A report of the most important results and records to be published when possible.

## 9<sup>th</sup> Item: International Training and Cooperation

**Article (A):**

In order to conserve the cultural and civilizational values of the local identity, local governments, authorities, groups and organizations must emphasis on the following:

**1-** Cultural programs to maintain principles of local character.

**2-** Training programs to support communities in maintaining traditional building systems, materials and craft skills.

**3-** Informational programs that enhance public awareness towards the local character, especially among the younger generations.

**4-** Establishment of national and regional networks dealing with local architecture to exchange expertise and experiences.

**5-** Specialized training should be provided for all those professions concerned with conservation.

**Article (B):**

The continuity of traditional building systems and craft skills associated with the local character is essential in presenting local

identity, maintaining its appearance during the repair and restoration of these structures. Such skills must be conserved, documented, supported and presented to the new generations of craftsmen and builders through education and training.

## 10th Item: Application and Responsible Authorities

Governments and responsible authorities should recognize the communities right to maintain their living traditions, and to protect them by all legislative, administrative, and financial means, and to hand them over to future generations. They should also acknowledge and implement all the international regulations related to preservation and restoration,  (such as Venice Charter of 1964, Washington Charter of 1987, Sofia Charter of  1996, New Mexico Charter of 1999, and others), which are considered as Integral parts of this Charter.

# Prize for preserve the architectural heritage identity of the cities

In order to encourage the Iraqi society to hold on the precious heritage value of Iraqi heritage cities and preserve its identity, The Preservation Center of Heritage and Identity of Iraqi Cities has decided to grant an annual prize for preserve of architectural heritage identity of the cities, for two buildings, the first one for an old heritage building maintained by its owners and the other one grants to a modern building was designed according to the architectural heritage theme that constitute the identity of the city.

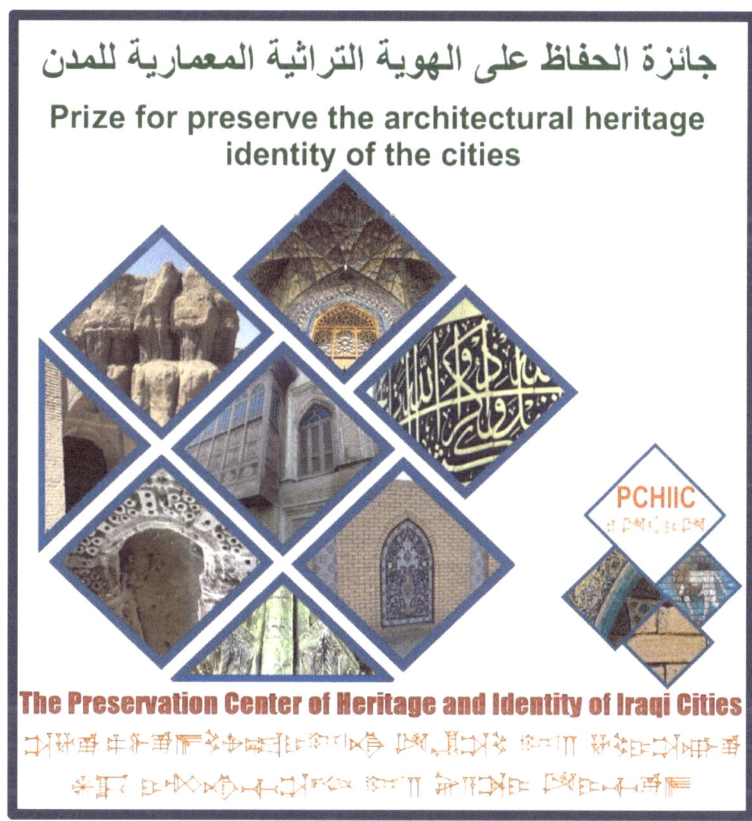

9 7 9 8 7 0 7 1 1 9 2 8 6